Cliff's Job

by Julianna Russell
illustrated by Chris Vallo

Practice Decodable 24

I0806510

McGraw Hill Education

Bothell, WA • Chicago, IL • Columbus, OH • New York, NY

MHEonline.com

Send all inquiries to:
McGraw-Hill Education
8787 Orion Place
Columbus, OH 43240-4027

ISBN: 978-0-02-136245-5
MHID: 0-02-136245-9

Printed in China.

8 9 10 11 12 DSS 27 26 25 24 23

Cliff has a job.
Cliff mops spots.

Cliff mops spots fast.
It is Cliff's job.

Cliff mops jam and milk spots.

Cliff did not miss a spot.

The dog has black spots.
Did Cliff mop him?

Cliff did not.

It is not Cliff's job.